SONGS OF
hope & restoration

ARRANGED FOR *ANY CHOIR*

BY MARTY PARKS

lillenas
PUBLISHING COMPANY

Contents

Blessed Be Your Name

The LORD gave and the LORD has taken away;
may the name of the LORD be praised. (Job 1:21 NIV)

Words and Music by
MATT REDMAN and
BETH REDMAN
Arr. by Marty Parks

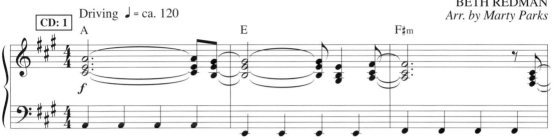

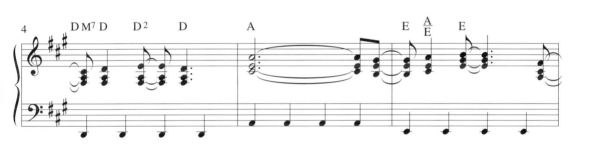

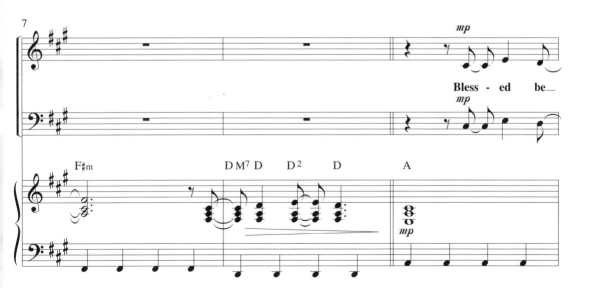

PLEASE NOTE: Copying of this product is NOT covered by CCLI licenses. For CCLI information call 1-800-234-2446.

6

Ev-'ry bless - ing You pour out I'll

turn back to praise! When the dark - ness

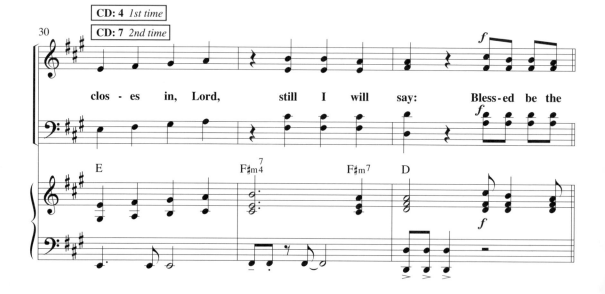

clos - es in, Lord, still I will say: Bless-ed be the

D.S. al Coda
(to pg. 8, meas. 25)

Except for Grace

If we confess our sins, he is faithful and just and will forgive us
our sins and purify us from all unrighteousness. (1 John 1:9 NIV)

Words and Music by
JEFF SILVEY
Arr. by Marty Parks

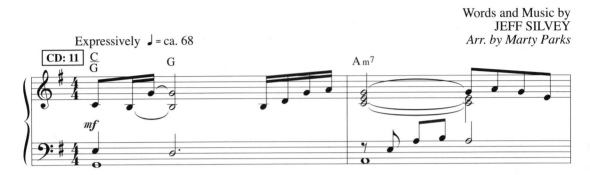

You've lost it all——— your dig-ni-ty— and pride—

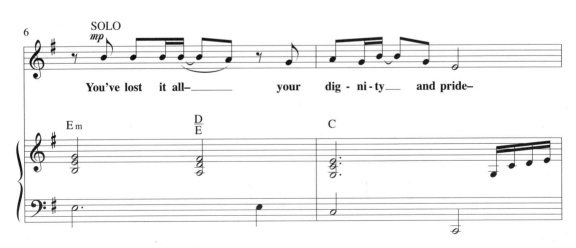

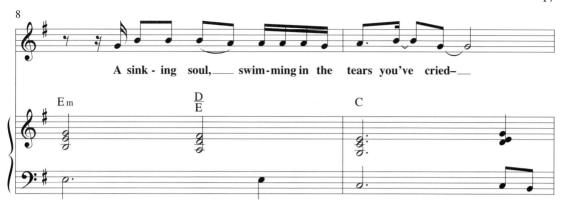

A sink - ing soul,___ swim-ming in the tears you've cried–___

Em   D/E   C

A - lone and help - less,   with - out a word___ to say,

Am7   G/B   C2

CD: 12

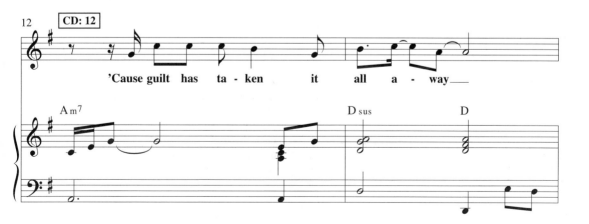

'Cause guilt has ta - ken   it   all   a - way___

Am7   Dsus   D

18

CD: 14

and a-fraid to dream. Sin has stripped us clean of
ev - 'ry-thing Ex -
place— ex - cept for grace. The

D.S. al Coda (to pg. 18, meas. 15)

SOLOIST joins CHOIR on melody

CODA

price is much_ too high for us_ to ev - er pay._

We could try for - ev - er and find no oth - er

way–_____ Ex -

23

24

I Will Sing

*Though the fig tree does not bud and there are no grapes
on the vines…yet I will rejoice in the LORD, I will be joyful
in God my Savior. (Habakkuk 3:17-18 NIV)*

Words and Music by
DON MOEN
Arr. by Marty Parks

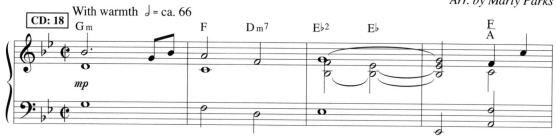

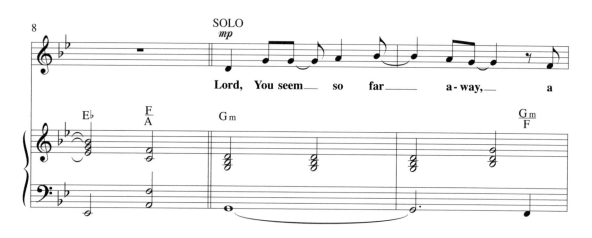

Lord, You seem____ so far____ a-way,____ a

28

30

34

Somebody Prayed for Me

With this in mind, we constantly pray for you...
(2 Thessalonians 1:11 NIV)

CLAIRE CLONINGER

ROBERT STERLING
Arr. by Marty Parks

PLEASE NOTE: Copying of this product is NOT covered by CCLI licenses. For CCLI information call 1-800-234-2446.

Some- bod - y prayed_____ for me._____

2. When the fu -

Say - ing what I____ could not say.____

Some - bod - y showed____ me the face____ of His mer - cy When

dark - ness was all____ I could see.____

Still

Be still and know that I am God; I will be exalted among the nations,
I will be exalted in the earth. (Psalm 46:10 NIV)

Words and Music by
REUBEN MORGAN
Arr. by Marty Parks

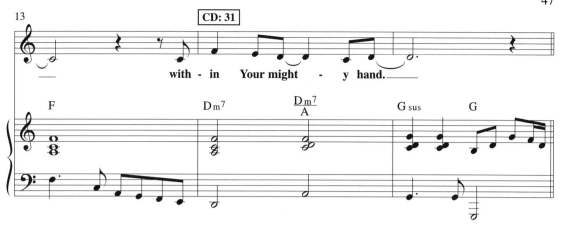

48

50

rise   and   thun - ders roar,_____   I   will   soar with

You   a - bove____   the storm.____   Fa - ther, You are

King   o - ver____   the flood;____   I   will   be   still,____

CD: 35 *1st time*

You are God!

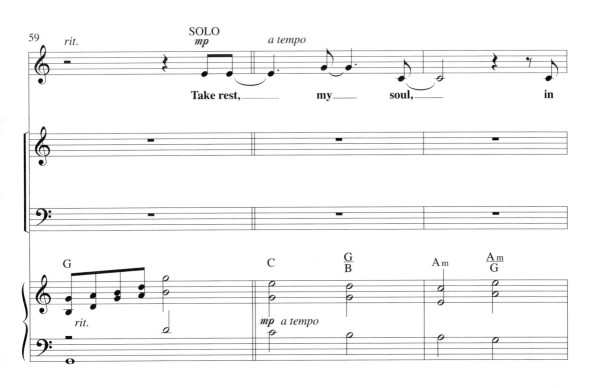

Take rest, my soul, in

Kingdom Prayer

The kingdom of God does not come with your careful observation...
the kingdom of God is within you. (Luke 17:20-21 NIV)

Words and Music by
DAN ADLER
Arr. by Marty Parks

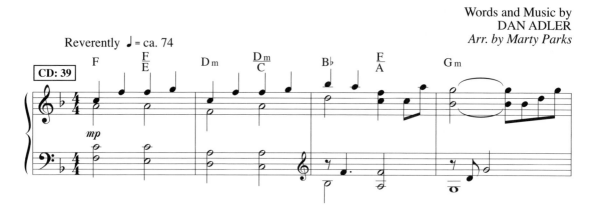

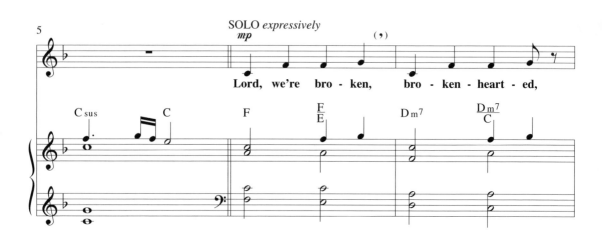

Lord, we're bro - ken, bro - ken - heart - ed,

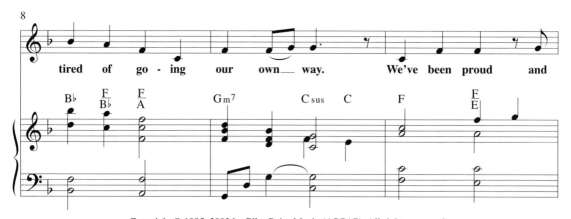

tired of go - ing our own_ way. We've been proud and

58

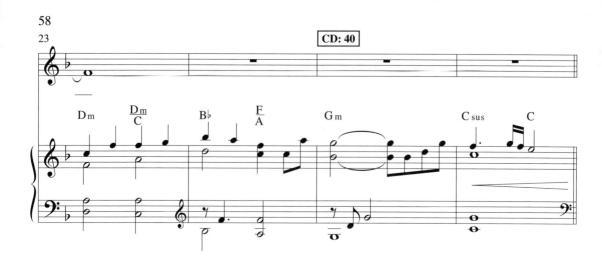

CD: 41

52
right - ful throne. Lord, we need Your pow'r with - in us,

D⁷sus D⁷ G/D G G/F♯ Em⁷ Am G/A D⁷ Am/G G

55
for we have none of our own. Take this hun - gry

Bm Em Asus Am Dsus D G G/F♯

CD: 42

58
heart and fill it with Thy pow'r and Thine a - lone.

Em⁷ G/D C G/C Am D⁷sus D⁷ G/D G G/F♯

62

Passionately

Lord, make us Your___ king - dom___ peo - ple, for we're noth - ing___

(cues optional)

on our___ own.___ Do Your will and bring Your king - dom;

fill our hearts and take___ Your throne.

CD: 43

63

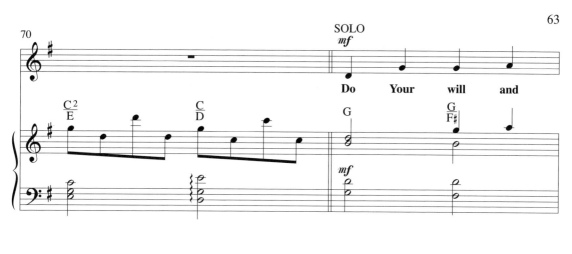

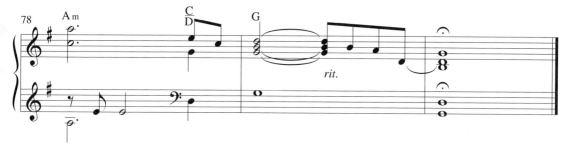

As We Worship You

He put a new song in my mouth, a hymn of praise to our God.
Many will see and fear and put their trust in the LORD.
(Psalm 40:3 NIV)

Words and Music by
TOMMY WALKER
Arr. by Marty Parks

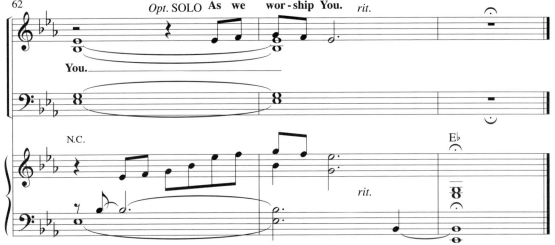

No Need to Fear

So do not fear, for I am with you; do not be dismayed for I am your God.
I will strengthen you and help you; I will uphold you
with my righteous right hand. (Isaiah 41:10 NIV)

Words and Music by
MARTY PARKS
Arr. by Marty Parks

He's lift-ing you up,_____ His love has re-deemed_

CD: 53

_ you. Your God is here,_____ there's no need to fear._

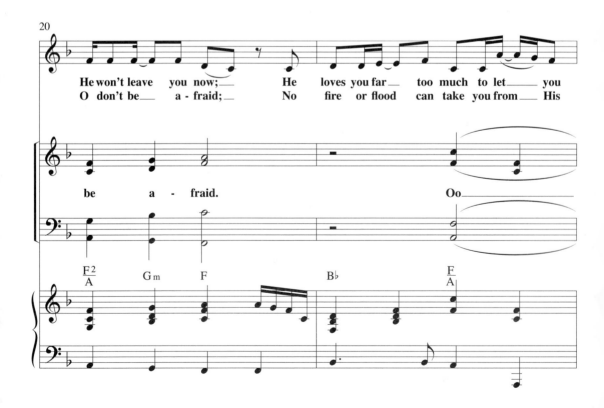

go.
So when you stand to tell the world your sto - ry
hand.
So put the past be-hind you, God's cre - a - ting

Oo

Gm B♭m6/D♭ C   A/C♯

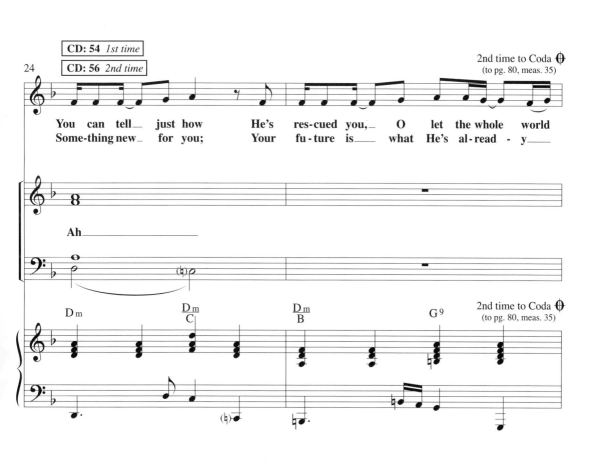

CD: 54 1st time
CD: 56 2nd time

2nd time to Coda
(to pg. 80, meas. 35)

You can tell just how He's res-cued you, O let the whole world
Some-thing new for you; Your fu-ture is what He's al-read - y

Ah

Dm   Dm/C   Dm/B   G9   2nd time to Coda
(to pg. 80, meas. 35)

He's lift-ing you up,_____ His love has re-deemed_

CD: 55

_____ you. Your God is here,_____ there's no need to fear._

He Giveth More Grace

But he said to me, "My grace is sufficient for you, for my power
is made perfect in weakness." Therefore I will boast all the more gladly
about my weaknesses, so that Christ's power may rest on me.
(2 Corinthians 12:9 NIV)

ANNIE JOHNSON FLINT

HUBERT MITCHELL
Arr. by Marty Parks

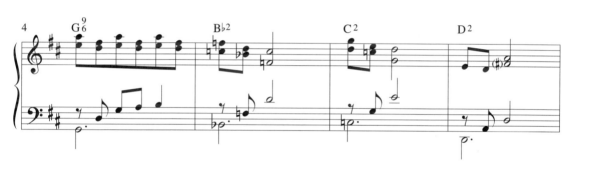

He giv-eth more grace when the

88

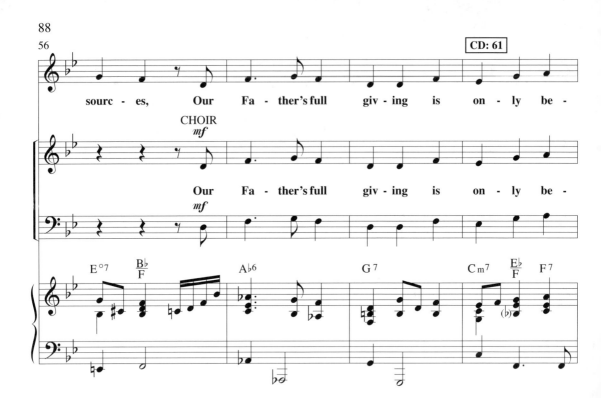

Just As I Am

Let us then approach the throne of grace with confidence,
so that we may receive mercy and find grace to help us
in our time of need. (Hebrews 4:16 NIV)

CHARLOTTE ELLIOTT

MARTY PARKS
Arr. by Marty Parks

O Lamb___ of God,___ I come,___ I come,___

___ I come.___ Lamb of God,___ I

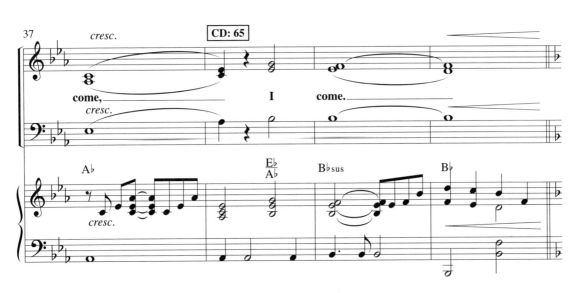

come,___ I come.___

98

Lamb of God,___ I___ come,___ I
come.___ Lamb of God,___ I___ come.___

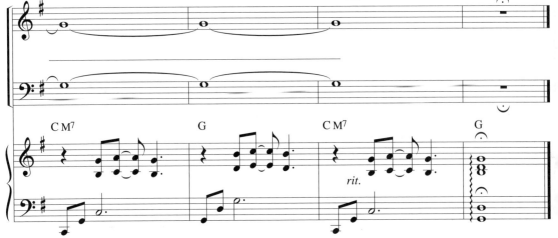

Jesus, Pray for Me

Therefore he is able to save completely those who come
to God through him, because he always lives
to intercede for them. (Hebrews 7:25 NIV)

Words and Music by
KENN MANN
Arr. by Marty Parks

108

Made Me Glad

Whom have I in heaven but you? And earth has nothing I desire
besides you. My flesh and my heart may fail, but God is the strength
of my heart and my portion forever. (Psalm 73:25-26 NIV)

Words and Music by
MIRIAM WEBSTER
Arr. by Marty Parks

I will___

PLEASE NOTE: Copying of this product is NOT covered by CCLI licenses. For CCLI information call 1-800-234-2446.

bless the Lord___ for - ev - - er.___

CD: 74

I will___ trust Him at___ all times.___

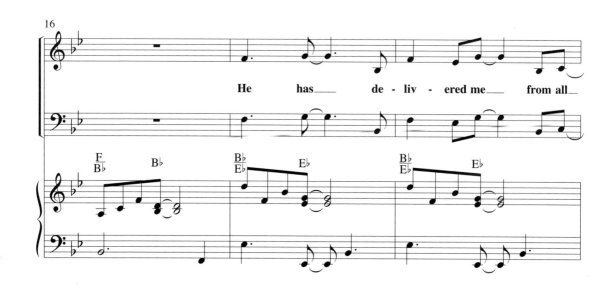

He has___ de - liv - ered me___ from all___

Also available . . .

Online Devotionals
for

*SONGS OF
HOPE & RESTORATION*

~~~~~~~~~~~~~~~~

Devotional thoughts, written by Marty Parks, to
accompany each of the choral arrangements in
SONGS OF HOPE & RESTORATION

~~~~~~~~~~~~~~~~

Use these inspirational comments in choir or worship team
rehearsals, choir newsletters, personal devotional times, or as
introductions in worship.

~~~~~~~~~~~~~~~~

Available as <u>free</u> downloads!

Go to www.lillenas.com!

SCRIPTS OF

HOPE &

RESTORATION

Hopeless…desperate…alone.
Just how does faith help us stand up in the face of tragedy?
What about the times that faith doesn't seem to make a difference?
How do we pray when really tough times hit us?
Can we admit that some of us choose not to pray?

God is working in the midst of our messy, doubt-filled and difficult
life experiences, but that's not always clear to us. We all experience
times when we need hope and restoration.

Ideally suited as companion pieces for the choral arrangements in
Songs of Hope & Restoration, these dramatic sketches and monologs
address our pain, our suffering, and the power of our God who sees it
all. Use them in worship, in retreat settings, or anywhere the
powerful message of hope and restoration is needed.

lillenas
PUBLISHING COMPANY

PO Box 419527
Kansas City, MO 64141

Topical Index

This index is a guide to help you find songs and scripts that relate to the listed themes.
The scripts (titles in quotes) are available in *Scripts of Hope & Restoration.*